T0143985

# The Lord Is My Shepherd

## 23rd Psalm
### *of* DAVID

## Melody Lafferty

AuthorHouse™
1663 Liberty Drive
Bloomington, IN 47403
www.authorhouse.com
Phone: 833-262-8899

This book is printed on acid-free paper.

Scripture quotations marked NKJV are taken from the New King James Version. Copyright © 1982 by Thomas Nelson, Inc. Used by permission. All rights reserved.

ISBN: 978-1-6655-4133-6 (sc)
       978-1-6655-4134-3 (e)

Print information available on the last page.

Published by AuthorHouse  10/14/2021

authorHOUSE®

# The Lord Is My Shepherd

## 23rd Psalm
### *of* DAVID

Scripture memorizing has never been easier for the 23rd Psalm of David.

Treat your child to a fun experience in learning God's word as Jesus leads us.

The colorful images of this book will capture the child's attention while learning of God's love and His great sense of humor.

This book plants scripture into the heart of the child which is a treasure they can draw upon their whole life.

*Melody Lafferty*

# The Lord Is My Shepherd

# I Shall Not Want

# He Makes Me Lie Down In Green Pastures

He Leads Me Beside The Still Waters

# He Restores My Soul

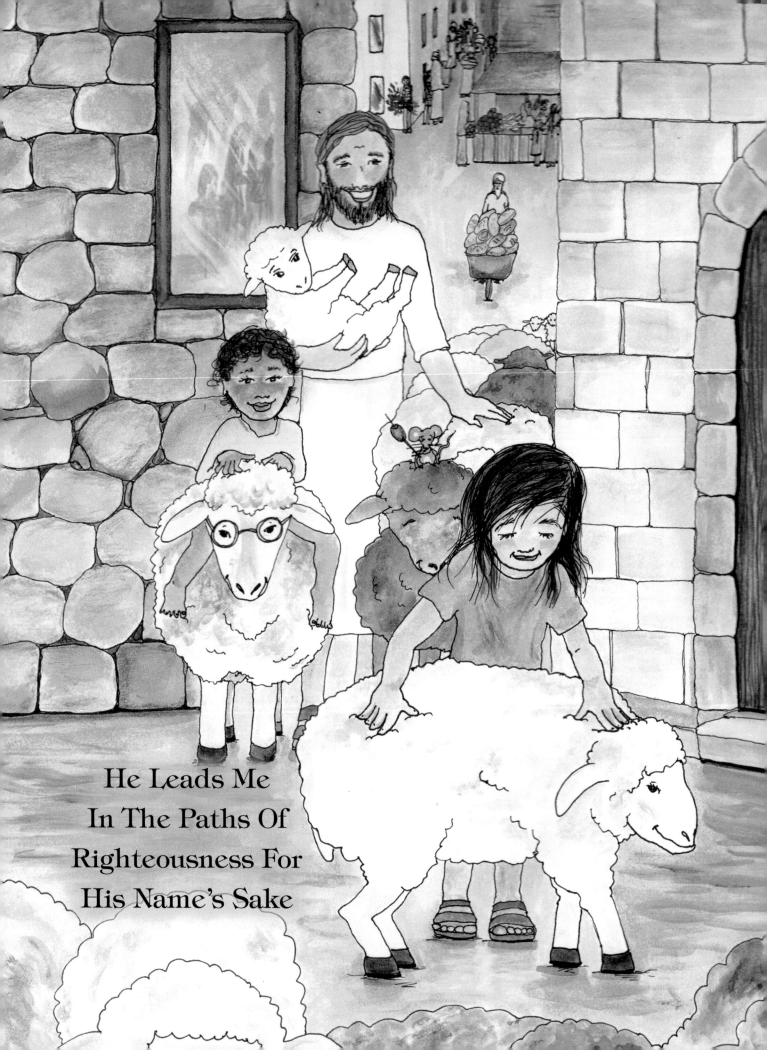

He Leads Me
In The Paths Of
Righteousness For
His Name's Sake

For You Are With Me, Your Rod And
Your Staff They Comfort Me.

You Anoint My Head With Oil

# My Cup Overflows

Surely Goodness and Mercy Will Follow
Me All The Days Of My Life

And I Will Dwell
In The House Of The Lord Forever

Amen

Printed in the United States
by Baker & Taylor Publisher Services